The

Shelagh Stephenson

Methuen Drama

Methuen Drama

1 3 5 7 9 10 8 6 4 2

Methuen Drama
A&C Black Publishers Ltd
36 Soho Square
London W1D 3QY
www.methuendrama.com

A CIP catalogue record for this book is available
from the British Library

ISBN: 978 1 408 11390 5

Typeset by Country Setting, Kingsdown, Kent
Printed and bound in Great Britain by
CPI Cox & Wyman, Reading, Berkshire

Synergy Theatre Project in association
with The Forgiveness Project
and Soho Theatre presents

the LONGROAD

By Shelagh Stephenson

Soho Theatre is supported by
ACE, Bloomberg, TEQUILA\London,
Westminster City Council, The City Bridge Trust

Performances in the Lorenz Auditorium
Registered Charity No: 267234

the LONGROAD
By Shelagh Stephenson

The Long Road was first performed at Soho Theatre on 19 May 2008 following a tour to London prisons and revived in November of the same year.

Cast
Mary **Denise Black**
John **Michael Elwyn**
Elizabeth **Alison Newman**
Emma **Michelle Tate**
Joe **Steven Webb**

Director **Esther Baker**
Designer **Katy McPhee**
Composer **Neil McArthur**
Lighting Designer **Tony Simpson**
Assistant Director **Francesca Seeley**
Casting Director **Nadine Hoare**
Lighting Technician **Adam Povey**
Stage Management **Ricky Copp** and **Carl Fletcher**
General Manager for Synergy **Jennie McClure**

Please note that the text of the play which appears in this volume may be changed during the rehearsal process and appear in a slightly altered form in performance.

Supported by
Peter De Haan Charitable Trust,
29th May 1961 Charitable Trust,
Metropolitan Police Service and Rev John Wates

foreword

This play was written to be performed in prisons as well as in theatres, and so I chose to write it in a particular, heightened style, in which the audience is often addressed directly. Much of the background understanding came from visits to prisons where, with people from The Forgiveness Project, and Synergy Theatre Project, we talked through notions of forgiveness and restorative justice with prisoners. Like most people, I had little prior knowledge of the prison system – well, none, to be precise. But I came to realise that almost all the people I met inside had been profoundly damaged, long before they ended up in jail. We all know this somewhere at the back of our brains, but the actual reality of it is shocking. None of the prisoners I met came from an even vaguely stable background: they were all bred from a chaotic and toxic mixture of familial neglect, criminality, and varying degrees of violence. Many of them had spent large portions of their adult lives in jail, and many of them moved me profoundly as they struggled to acknowledge and understand the effects of their crimes. They also made me laugh, and being the sort of playwright I am, this was something of a relief. I dedicate the play to all those prisoners taking their first faltering footsteps towards redemption and understanding, and all those victims who choose to meet them on the road.

Shelagh Stephenson

Synergy Theatre Project, in collaboration with The Forgiveness Project, commissioned **The Long Road** following a period of research in London prisons with Shelagh Stephenson.

DENISE BLACK MARY

Denise is probably best known as hairdresser Denise Osbourne in **Coronation Street,** Denny's mad bad mum in **Bad Girls,** and Hazel in **Queer As Folk.** Other recent TV credits include: **Robin Hood, Doc Marten, To The Ends Of The Earth, Born and Bred, Waking The Dead, The Vice, The Second Coming, The Scarlet Pimpernel, Clocking Off, Sins, Midsomer Murders, Serious and Organized, A Good Thief, Macbeth, The Bill, Doctors** and **Casualty.** Also Fred Schepsi's film **Last Orders.** Denise's recent theatre credits include: **Aristo** (Chichester Festival Theatre), **The Seagull** (Royal Court Theatre), Martha in **Who's Afraid Of Virginia Woolf** (Liverpool Playhouse), Mrs Bryant in **Roots** and title roles in **Yerma** and **Mrs Warren's Profession** (Manchester Royal Exchange), **The Mistress** (The Sherman), **The Woman Who Cooked Her Husband** (Nottingham Playhouse and Plymouth Theatre Royal), and Goneril of that woeful line 'pluck out his eyes' in **King Lear** at the Ludlow Festival.

MICHAEL ELWYN JOHN

Michael's recent theatre credits include: **Three Sisters** (Manchester Royal Exchange), **The Woman Hater** (Orange Tree), **What Every Woman Knows** (Manchester Royal Exchange), **The Solid Gold Cadillac** (Garrick), **Darwin In Malibu** (Birmingham Rep), **Revelations** (Hampstead Theatre), **Broken Glass** (West Yorkshire Playhouse) and tours of **Strangers On A Train, Vertigo** and **Otherwise Engaged.** His recent television includes Sir Edward in **Robin Hood, U Be Dead, 10 Days To War, Churchill at War, Suez, Sharpe's Challenge, Midsomer Murders, Dirty Filthy Love, Daniel Deronda, Bad Girls, North Square, Border Café, Stagestruck, Micawber, Silent Witness, This Life, The Brief** and, of course, **The Bill.** Films include **Surveillance, Shadowman, Jinnah, Dot The i, Half Moon Street, The French Lieutenant's Woman, A Touch Of Class** and **Decline and Fall.**

ALISON NEWMAN ELIZABETH

Alison's theatre credits include: **Vagina Monologues** (West End & Tour), **The Lying Kind** (Royal Court), **Night Of The Soul** (RSC), **Luminosity** (RSC), **Loveplay** (RSC), **Smile** (Soho Theatre), **The Games Room** (Soho Theatre), **The Censor** (Royal Court/The Red Room), and **The Tempest** (Royal Exchange). Her TV credits include: **Open Wide, Rocket Man, Hex, Eastenders, Footballers' Wives, The Prince and the Pauper, Casualty, Bad Girls, The Bill, Touching Evil, Great Expectations** and **Butterfly Collectors,** and films: **Kidulthood** and **Ashes and Sand.**

MICHELLE TATE EMMA

Michelle trained at Drama Centre and her theatre credits include: **The Big Lie** (RSC at Latitude Festival), **Chatroom/Citizenship** (National Theatre, UK tour and Hong Kong Arts Festival); **Martha, Josie and the Chinese Elvis** and **The Crucible** (Birmingham Repertory Theatre); **The Father** (Chichester Festival Theatre); **Jane Eyre** (Manchester Royal Exchange

Studio) and **Essex Girls** for Open House (The Royal Court). Her radio work includes: **The Casebook of Inspector Steine** and **Betsy and Napoleon** (both for BBC Radio 4), and TV: **Sugar Rush, Bleak House, Casualty, The Bill** and **Harry Hill's TV Burp**. Michelle also starred in a short film, **The Toughest Girl in the World** and the feature **Dread.**

STEVEN WEBB JOE

Steven's work in theatre includes: **Sh*t-M*x** (Trafalgar Studios), **Sons of York** (Finborough Theatre), **Chatroom/Citizenship** (National Theatre/UK tour/Hong Kong Arts Festival), **The History Boys** (National Theatre/UK Tour/West End), **On The Shore Of The Wide World** (National Theatre and Royal Exchange, Manchester), **Kes** (Royal Exchange, Manchester), **A Midsummer Night's Dream** (Sheffield Crucible), **The Trestle At Pope Lick Creek** (Southwark Playhouse), **Dark Of The Moon** (King's Head), **Oliver!** (West End) **Scrooge, Twopence to Cross the Mersey** and **Her Benny** (Liverpool Empire). His TV includes: **After Sun, Mr Harvey Lights a Candle, Loving You, The Inspector Lynley Mysteries, Bad Girls, Peak Practice, The Rainbow Room, Anything's Possible, The Magicians House** (Series 2) and **Heart Of Gold.** And his film work includes: **Nobody's Perfect, To Kill a King, Thou Shalt Not Kill, Wives & Daughters** and **A Christmas Cracker.** Radio: **Phaeton, Another Country, The Arab-Israeli Cookbook, To Sir With Love, Chronicles Of Narnia,** Peter Pan in **Scarlet, Ah! Wilderness, Stalingrad Kiss** and **The Accountant.**

SHELAGH STEPHENSON WRITER

Shelagh Stephenson has written extensively for radio, theatre, television and film. Her stage plays include: **The Memory of Water** (Hampstead, West End, New York) which won an Olivier Award in 2000, and is performed all over the world; **An Experiment with an Air Pump** (Royal Exchange, Hampstead, New York) which won the Peggy Ramsay Award; **Ancient Lights** (Hampstead); **Five Kinds of Silence** (Lyric Hammersmith, Writers Guild Award); **Mappa Mundi** (National Theatre). She is currently writing plays for Hampstead Theatre, Live Theatre (Newcastle), Atlantic Theatre (New York), and **In the Same Boat**, a pilot series for Lime Pictures.

ESTHER BAKER DIRECTOR

Esther is the Artistic Director of Synergy Theatre Project which works with prisoners and ex-prisoners. She has worked extensively in prisons for the past 14 years and co-founded Synergy in 1999 soon after winning the Butler Trust Development Award for 'an outstanding contribution to the effective care of prisoners'. She has directed thirteen of Synergy's productions, and her work includes: **Elmina's Kitchen** (HMP Brixton), **On the Waterfront** (Wimbledon Studio Theatre), **Burn** and **Someone to Watch Over Me** (Southwark Playhouse), **Accidental Death of an Anarchist** (HMP Wandsworth), **The Memory of Water** (HMP Downview), **Respect, Guilty by Association** and **Gunpoint** (HMP Latchmere House and schools tour), **Dealer's Choice** (Orange Tree), **A Memory of Two Mondays** (Cockpit), **Write Now** rehearsed readings (Royal Court), **Inferno** (Young Vic Studio), **The Lieutenant of Inishmore** (Assistant Director at the Garrick). She has trained and worked at National Theatre Studio. Her first short film **The Rains of Fear** was screened at BFI Southbank and LA and Krakow Film Festivals.

KATY MCPHEE SET DESIGNER

Katy McPhee trained at Wimbledon School of Art, gaining a BA Hons in Theatre Design. She has designed costumes for dance including DV8 Physical Theatre on four productions. Katy's TV credits include: **The History of Venice** (BBC1), **The Power of Art** (BBC2), **Pinochet in Suburbia** (BBC2) and **Consenting Adults** (BBC1). Recent projects include production design and costume design for **Vera Brittain**, a drama documentary to be shown on BBC1 as part of the Armistice Day celebrations. At present she is designing costumes for a production in Madrid for Rakata Theatre Company, **Fuente Ovejuna** by Lope de Vega. She also occasionally styles Paul McCartney.

NEIL McARTHUR COMPOSER

Neil is a prolific artist. His work spans the West End, Broadway and the international stage, including Olivier Award-winning and Tony Nominated **Five Guys Named Moe**. He has worked at the National Theatre on **A Streetcar Named Desire** and **Elmina's Kitchen** among others and has run workshops at the National Theatre Studio. His TV credits are extensive and Neil appeared on **The Jazz Album** with Simon Rattle while other recordings (**Five Guys Named Moe** and **Blues in the Night**) have achieved Gold and Silver Discs respectively. His recent work includes **Maria Friedman: Rearranged** at the Menier Chocolate Factory.

TONY SIMPSON LIGHTING DESIGNER

Tony's work includes: **Bat Boy, Ying Tong, Members Only, Missing Persons, Berkoff's Women, Cooking with Elvis, Round the Horne... Revisited** and **Under the Doctor** (all West End); **Steptoe and Son** (UK Tour); **The Lesson, The Merchant of Venice** (The Arcola); **Blue Orange** (Watford Palace); **The Flu Season, Habitats** (The Gate); **The Man Who** (Orange Tree Theatre); **The Way of The World, The Weir, Waiting for Godot, Arcadia** (Royal Theatre Northampton); **Master Harold... and the Boys, Burn, Someone Who'll Watch Over Me** (Southwark Playhouse); **On The Waterfront** (Wimbledon Studio); **Small Miracle, Death of a Salesman, She Stoops to Conquer, Miss Julie, A Midsummer Night's Dream, Betrayal, Our Country's Good,** (Mercury Theatre, Colchester); **Romeo and Juliet** (Nuffield Theatre, Southampton). As Associate in the West End: the National Theatre's **Life x 3** and **An Inspector Calls** (also various UK Tours); **Who's Afraid of Virginia Woolf, The Shape of Things, Patsy Cline – The Musical, Amadeus** (also New York, Los Angeles) and tours of **The Woman in Black; The Weir** (also Sicily and Australia), **Hobson's Choice** and has toured with the RSC, Welsh National Opera and the Royal Opera House. Further details at www.tonysimpson.com

Synergy Theatre Project, established in 1999, works with prisoners and ex-prisoners through theatre towards resettlement and rehabilitation whilst placing the wider issues surrounding imprisonment in the public arena. Its work is founded on the belief that theatre can be transformative and challenges perceptions of both prisoners and society, building a more positive future.

At the heart of Synergy's work lie theatre productions with prisoners and ex-prisoners which can have a profound effect on both participants and audiences. Synergy's other strands of activity comprise new writing, including national prison script writing competitions and professional commissions, and a crime prevention programme involving prisoners and ex-prisoners touring productions and workshops about crime-related issues to schools and Youth Offending Teams. These projects give prisoners a voice, develop skills and create training and employment to support social re-integration.

The Long Road meets one of Synergy's central aims to raise awareness of issues relating to the criminal justice system, and it is intended to be the first of many commissions by the company.

The **forgiveness** project

The Forgiveness Project is a UK charity that explores forgiveness, reconciliation and conflict resolution through real-life human experience. It uses stories, and in particular its powerful exhibition, **The F Word**, to open up dialogue and promote understanding. Many of those voices celebrated in the exhibition and on the website, also share their stories in person. The project works in prisons, schools, faith communities, and with any group wishing to explore the nature of forgiveness, whether in the wider political context or within their own lives. The organisation has no religious affiliations.

In the past four years, The Forgiveness Project has toured **The F Word** exhibit to over 300 venues worldwide reaching up to 50,000 people; the website receives on average 500 visitors a day, many emailing words of support, some telling of their own trauma and how reading/hearing the stories has helped them deal with pain in their own lives. The project aims to facilitate a dialogue about forgiveness, both in personal relationships and within the criminal justice system, by generating widespread media coverage and providing workshops and materials for schools and prisons. The Forgiveness Project prison workshops use personal testimonies, life-lines, film, and discussion in both large and small groups to explore what forgiveness and restorative justice mean both generally and individually. It involves listening to real personal stories of loss and abuse and learning how people can be transformed by forgiveness. It is stressed that no one is obliged to forgive and the point of the workshop is to engage in a personal exploration of forgiveness. As one prisoner put it after being on the workshop, "it allows you to come to terms with yourself, so that you can come to terms with what you've done to others".

www.theforgivenessproject.com

Why me?

VICTIMS FOR RESTORATIVE JUSTICE

Collaborating with Synergy and The Forgiveness Project on the revival of **The Long Road**, Why Me? is a new victim-led organisation founded in May 2008, presently under the auspices of the Restorative Justice Consortium. It specifically campaigns for restorative justice to be made available for all and for the experience of victims in the Criminal Justice process to be improved. Why Me? was born of one man's story. Will Riley, Chair of Why Me?, was burgled and attacked in 2002 by Peter Woolf, a career criminal. They met two months later through a Restorative Justice conference in Pentonville Prison, an event that changed both their lives.

www.why-me.org

PERFORMANCE PROVOCATIVE AND COMPELLING THEATRE, COMEDY AND CABARET
TALKS VIBRANT DEBATES ON CULTURE, THE ARTS AND THE WAY WE LIVE
SOHO CONNECT A THRIVING EDUCATION, COMMUNITY AND OUTREACH PROGRAMME
WRITERS' CENTRE DISCOVERING AND NURTURING NEW WRITERS AND ARTISTS
SOHO THEATRE BAR SERVING TASTY, AFFORDABLE FOOD AND DRINK FROM 12PM TILL LATE.

'The capital's centre for daring international drama.'
EVENING STANDARD

'A jewel in the West End'
BBC LONDON

THE TERRACE BAR
Drinks can be taken into the auditorium and are available from
the Terrace Bar on the second floor.

SOHO THEATRE ONLINE
Giving you the latest information and previews of upcoming shows,
Soho Theatre can be found on facebook, myspace and youtube as well as
at sohotheatre.com

EMAIL INFORMATION LIST
For regular programme updates and offers visit sohotheatre.com/mailing

HIRING THE THEATRE
Soho Theatre has a range of rooms and spaces for hire. Please contact the
theatre on 020 7287 5060 or go to sohotheatre.com/hires for further details.

THE SOHO THEATRE DEVELOPMENT CAMPAIGN

Soho Theatre receives core funding from Arts Council England, London. In order to provide as diverse a programme as possible and expand our audience development and outreach work, we rely upon additional support from trusts, foundations, individuals and businesses.

We sincerely thank all our principal sponsors:
Anonymous, Tony and Rita Gallagher, Nigel Gee, Roger Jospe, Jack and Linda Keenan, Sigrid Rausing, Carolyn Ward, The Harold Hyam Wingate Foundation, The Rose Foundation, The Ernest Cook Trust, Man Group plc Charitable Trust and Goodman Derrick.

To find out how to become a Friend of Soho Theatre, contact the development department on **020 7478 0143**, or visit **sohotheatre.com**.

21 Dean Street, London W1D 3NE sohotheatre.com
Admin: 020 7287 5060 Box Office: 020 7478 0100

Artistic Director: **Lisa Goldman**
Executive Director: **Mark Godfrey** (sabbatical)
Acting Executive Director: **Catherine Thornborrow**

The Long Road

Characters

Joe, *twenty*
Mary, *his mother, fifty-two*
John, *her husband*
Emma Price, *eighteen*
Elizabeth, *late thirties*

The style of the piece is heightened. It requires the bare
minimum of naturalistic settings and props.

An almost bare stage. The backdrop is a huge, grainy photograph of a young boy of eighteen, Danny, smiling into the camera.

Joe, *twenty, enters, walks into a dim spotlight.*

Joe It wasn't even late. Ten o'clock or something. There were people around, masses of them. I went into a shop to get some cigarette papers and when I came out I saw this girl give Danny a punch in the chest, and I said hey, and she looked round and her eyes were black, no colour in them, and I thought she's on something. And as I was thinking this, she walked off, didn't run, she just strolled, and I saw Danny crumple as if all his bones had melted. He didn't make a sound, it wasn't dramatic, not like a film, and I thought he was joking, but at the same time I knew he wasn't because there was something weird about the way he just folded up. People walked past him, one guy even stepped over him, most people didn't notice because it didn't look serious. I went to him and knelt down and there was blood on his shirt, a little round mark over his heart. It was nothing, a tiny nick, but as I held him it spread out like a big red chrysanthemum. A guy came over and said what happened I'm a nurse and I said I don't know is he going to be all right? His face went from normal to the colour of paper right in front of my eyes. He went from being alive to being dead in that instant. I couldn't believe it, I'd never seen anyone dead before except our dog Tansy and it's not the same with an animal, but I knew he was dead, I saw the life drain out of him and his head was in my hands and I was shouting fucking hell somebody do something, and the guy who was the nurse gave him mouth-to-mouth which he must have known was a waste of time but I think he did it for me, to say look, I'm doing something, I'm doing the best I can. Then an ambulance came. I don't know who called it. Police all over the place. Sirens, blue lights. People were still going into bars, dodging round police cars, having a quick glance as they walked past, people who were still alive, like he'd been a minute ago. How could he slip from one state to the other in the blink of an eye? I couldn't take it in: life and death so banged up against each other, so close there's not a hair's breadth between them. I thought this is not happening,

I thought how am I going to tell Mum? If I hadn't taken him into town that night, if we hadn't gone to Soho, if I hadn't gone into the shop for papers, he would still be alive. Someone else would probably be dead because she was fucking nuts, the girl who did it, but I don't care about those other people because I don't know them and Danny was my brother and now every single thing is totally fucked, for ever.

The lights fade down slightly on **Joe** *as his mother,* **Mary**, *fifty-two, walks into her own dim spotlight. He remains onstage, lit, but in shadow.*

Mary   I'd fallen asleep in front of the television and the doorbell rang. I was a bit bleary, I had no idea what time it was. I was expecting it to be the boys, forgotten their key. I had no premonition, nothing like that. John was away, but I wasn't afraid, I wasn't expecting anything bad at all. But as soon as I opened the door and saw the policemen, I thought oh no. It's John. He's been in an accident. He's had a heart attack. Or has there been a bomb somewhere? They were very nice, the police, they came in, I don't remember exactly what they said, it's all a blur, are you Daniel Pritchard's mother, something like that, and of course you know it's bad, they don't send policemen round lightly, they don't have the manpower. The moment they said his name, there was a roaring sound at the back of my head and I knew. I think I said where's Joe, I suddenly felt very panicky about Joe, but they said he's fine, Joe's fine, which could only mean that Dan wasn't. But I didn't want them to say it, I didn't want to know. I felt I was balancing on the edge of something, as if my life had a hinge in it, and I was about to step into some dark other place, and I didn't want to go there. All this must have happened over a matter of seconds but it felt longer than that, everything stretched out like elastic, because in these tiny fragments of time huge, inconceivable things were happening, the world was changed in an instant. So I kept saying would you like a cup of tea because I was trying to stave off the moment when they might tell me Dan was dead, because as long as they didn't say it, it hadn't happened. I realise this is ridiculous. Even when they did say it, I don't remember hearing it. And I wanted to see Joe very badly but they said he'd collapsed, the shock tumbled him over, so he was still at the hospital. They kept telling me to sit down but I couldn't because sitting down somehow meant taking it in and I didn't want to take it in. I wanted to hop back into the moment before they arrived at my door, when my life was just fine, and I was innocent and Danny was still alive. I'd still like to do that but it would be more than a hop now, it would be a long, long crawl, back through all those days and weeks and months. One day he will have been dead for more days than he lived. He lived for six thousand six hundred and ninety-three days, and I saw him for almost every one of them. It's strange, the things you think of, how many weeks, days, hours, minutes did he live, this is what goes through your head when you can't sleep. Sheep-counting for the bereaved. It doesn't work though. You still can't sleep.

The lights fade down slightly on **Mary** *as her husband* **John** *enters and walks into his own dim spotlight. She remains onstage, lit, but in shadow.*

John   I've taken up running. I needed to stop thinking so I used to trot round the block. Then two blocks. Two miles. Ten miles. Twenty miles. Before it happened I couldn't run for a bus. Now I could do a marathon. Not that I would, because it would involve other people and I'm not interested in that. I like pounding the pavements at night, alone, with my heart pumping, and the blood roaring in my head, drowning out all the stuff. If I didn't have to go to work I would run all day. When I'm out there I don't think about what happened, although it's always there somewhere, but mostly I'm thinking how to get through the next mile. I know what it is, I'm not stupid, I know I'm in flight. Some people drink, some of them sleep all the time, some of them take drugs. I run. We're all in flight from the thing that's too hard to bear. With me, I'm also avoiding talking to people, because I've noticed since it happened that no one knows what to say to you. Or they think you want to talk about it all the time, and actually I don't have the words. This one particular woman, she said to us, at least God is looking after him now and I thought why the fuck wasn't God looking after him before it happened? Why did he have to die to get God's attention? But most of the time I don't have the words. I'm just hollowed out, like an empty cupboard.

In the daytime, when I walk down the street, I feel I've got a
flag on top of my head, saying *the man whose son was murdered*.
I've seen people cross the road to avoid me. I don't blame them,
it must be like talking to an open wound. All we want to be is
normal again, not murmured about, all those furtive glances,
I can't stand the pity. But normal's over, we know that, there's
a new normal now. We tried counselling. A woman with purple
nail varnish, and on her left hand she had a silver ring – a
heart with a dagger through it. I thought that's my heart she's
wearing, and it seemed a bit insensitive of her. Mary says I'm
imagining it, she never noticed any ring. Anyway she was
rubbish, the counsellor. Nothing can make this better. Have
you noticed they're always saying what can we learn from this
tragedy, or that one, as if having your son stabbed to death by
a total stranger might be part of a GCSE module called what
we can learn from random acts of pointless violence? I think of
all the things we taught him, the tricks of the trade: don't take
sweets from strangers, look right and left before you cross,
avoid recreational drugs which involve syringes, scoutmasters
who want to share your sleeping bag, use a condom, be aware.
And we failed him. Our eighteen years of raising went for
nothing, because death came out of nowhere for no reason.
There's no meaning to it, there's nothing to be learnt. At three
o'clock in the morning, that's what envelops me like a shroud:
I can't find any meaning in it at all . . .

Lights fade down slightly as **Emma** *enters and walks into her own dim
spotlight. The others remain onstage, lit, but in shadow, like a chorus.*

Emma   Everybody hates me. It doesn't bother me. I'm used
to it. My mum my dad my sisters brothers my nan grandad
uncles aunties neighbours people I've never even met. They all
hate me. I can't remember anything about it, I was out of it.
I only asked him for a quid, because I'd had my bag nicked
and how was I supposed to get home I didn't have the tube
fare and anyway I only needed a quid. That's all. I never asked
him for twenty quid or anything. One quid. I said can you lend
me a quid mate, and he said no fuck off, didn't even look at me.
He could've just given me the money. It was only a quid. One
pound fifty, something like that. Then I could've got the tube.

Could've gone home and everyone would've been fine. He shouldn't have spoke to me like that. I can't remember anything else. I was out of it. It was only a quid. Something like that.

The light changes so that **Joe**, **Mary** *and* **John** *are lit like a painting.*

Joe   We left the house together, but I came back alone.

Mary   On the table next to his bed, a cup of tea, half drunk –

John   Two books, half read.

Joe   The pillow still indented from his head.

Mary   His voice undeleted on the answerphone.

John   'We'll be back around one.'

Joe   The house had never seemed so full of him.

Mary   In those hours afterwards.

John   Every room vibrated with him.

Joe   Everything you touched had been touched by him –

Mary   Raw, and fresh, and sharp.

John   Not rubbed away by time.

Joe   He was more present than he'd ever been.

Mary   And absolutely gone.

John   This huge clanging absence, filling the house like a bell.

Mary   A cousin of mine, Jane. She said I couldn't go through what you're going through. I couldn't do it.

John   But it's not as if you have a choice, is it?

Joe   What would she have done? Died?

Mary   Because the problem is you don't die. You go on. One minute follows another. Monday becomes Tuesday becomes Wednesday becomes a week. You put one foot in front of the other.

John   You can't put the brake on and say stop.

Joe   We asked a doctor –

Mary   Who knew these things –

John   Would it have hurt him?

Joe   Would he feel any pain?

Mary   He shook his head.

John   But how would he know?

Joe   He'd never been stabbed through the heart.

Mary   He said adrenalin kicks in.

John   Fight or flight. A huge surge of hormones.

Joe   He said an antelope felled by a tiger doesn't feel pain.

Mary   Feels calm, in fact.

John   Dreamy.

Joe   Like slipping into a warm bath.

Mary   A moment of fear, then a cocoon of relief.

John   Acceptance.

Joe   Something about endorphins.

Mary   I said this is all well and good –

John   We realise you're trying to be helpful.

Joe   But Dan wasn't a fucking antelope.

Blackout.

Light on **Mary** *and* **Joe**. **Mary** *is reading a newspaper.*

Mary   Have you seen this?

Joe   What?

Mary   It's her.

Joe   What?

Mary (*showing him a photo in the article she's reading*)   Who's that?

Joe (*glancing at it*)   I dunno.

Mary   It's her.

Joe   Who?

Mary   Look at it properly.

He looks.

Joe   I still don't know.

Mary   Not that one. That's a woman called Elizabeth McKellan who's doing some workshop or other. In prisons.

Joe   I'm on my way out, Mum.

Mary   That one there. Look at her.

Joe   I am looking.

Mary   That is the person who killed Dan.

Joe   How can you tell?

Mary   Something about the tilt of her head, I'd recognise it anywhere.

Joe   They've blurred their faces, so you can't identify them. Pixelated.

Mary   What?

Joe   That's what it's called. Pixelated.

Mary   Well, that's her. Sitting there, alive. Doing a workshop, while Danny's dead.

Joe *looks more closely at the photo.*

Joe   I dunno, maybe . . .

Mary   What is she doing laughing, while Danny's dead?

Joe   How d'you know she's laughing? You can't see her face properly.

Mary   How can she be there, functioning as normal, when he's dead?

Joe   I'm meeting some people, Mum. I'm going to be late.

Mary   (*reading from the article*)   ' . . . working with women prisoners, to help them understand the narrative of their lives.' They'll be offering them aromatherapy next. All-expenses-paid trips to health farms in Thailand.

Joe   I'm going, OK?

Mary   The person who killed your brother is sitting around at workshops telling her life story.

Joe   I don't care what she does, Mum, because I don't give a fuck about her, OK? Stop reading this shit. Stop torturing yourself.

He takes the paper from her and throws it down.

See you later.

He goes out. Spotlight on **Mary**. *She goes to retrieve the paper.*

Mary   But I couldn't stop thinking about her. I put the article in my desk drawer, tucked away like a love letter. And every so often I'd get it out and stare at the photo of Emma Price, as if it might hold the answer to something. I was willing her to turn round, to look me in the eye, so I could say to her *Why did you do it?*

Blackout.

Lights up stage right on **Joe**.

Joe   You know in American films when tragedy strikes and the family all hold each other and sob and say I love you Mom, I love you Dad? Why didn't we do that? Our family just imploded. We went from four people to three people and the balance is all screwed up. There's a space where there used to be a person and you can't fill it. My dad, he never cried once,

not as far as I know, not in front of me, and that's not because
he didn't love Dan, he did, he loved him more than me, they
both did. Dan was their favourite. They say that's not true but
it is. I'm cool with it. I've always known it. These are the things
that Dan was: clever, funny, handsome, witty, graceful, charming,
affectionate, and now he's dead these things are written in
stone. They will never alter, they can never be contradicted.
He was only eighteen, he didn't have time to fuck up.

Lights up stage left on **John**, *in an armchair, with a glass of whisky and
a bottle next to him.*

John   You shouldn't have left him on the street at that time
of night.

Joe   It was ten o'clock, Dad.

John   What were you doing in the shop anyway?

Joe   Buying something. What else would I be doing?

John   What?

Joe   What d'you mean what?

John   What were you buying?

Joe   Papers. I was buying papers.

John   Papers?

Joe   Cigarette papers.

John   What were you going to do with them?

Joe   I was going to make a papier mâché model of the Taj
Mahal.

John   You were going to roll joints.

Joe   Whatever.

John   Don't whatever me, your brother's dead –

Joe   And I didn't kill him –

John   If you hadn't been buying papers to roll joints –

Joe   Spliffs.

John   What?

Joe   Nobody says joints. It could have been a can of Coke, it could have been anything. She would still have been outside. She would still have had a knife. And he would still be –

John   I'm not blaming you –

Joe   You are blaming me.

Mary *comes in with* **Elizabeth***, late thirties.*

Mary   This is Elizabeth McKellan.

Elizabeth   Have I come at a bad moment?

John   Are you from victim support?

Elizabeth   No –

John   Because they're a bunch of arses.

Joe   I'm off. He's pissed, by the way.

He starts to go.

Mary   Joe, stay, please.

John   Anybody can go on a two-week course and come out a *trained counsellor* which just means they can hang around your house drinking tea and saying how are you feeling now and why do they say *trained counsellors*? Is there an untrained variety?

Elizabeth   Well, I'm not a counsellor so you're OK –

John   We don't need anyone else saying how does that make you feel and you must be very angry, they say it in that mincing little Horlicks voice, just add hot milk, God, I fucking hate them –

He pours himself another drink.

Mary   Elizabeth has been working with prisoners. She met the girl . . . she met Emma Price.

Pause.

John   Sorry?

Elizabeth   Emma Price. She met her.

John   I don't understand.

Mary   I want us to talk about it −

John   About what?

Joe   Mum, I don't think you need this at the moment −

Mary   Don't tell me what I need, you have no idea what I need.

Elizabeth   I thought you'd told them I was coming?

John   Somebody tell me what's going on here.

Mary   I asked Elizabeth to come because there's something come into our lives that we can't talk about −

Joe   We never fucking stop talking about him −

Mary   I don't mean Dan. I mean her.

John   Who's *her*?

Mary   The girl who did it. Emma Price. You must think about her.

John   I don't. I refuse to.

Mary   Oh for God's sake, she may as well have moved in with us −

John   She murdered our son.

Mary   I know, but −

John   But what?

Mary   She can't just be − there must be more to her than that −

John   What's does it have to do with us, what she is or what she isn't?

Mary   I need to understand –

John   No. You want it to mean something. But it doesn't.

He gets up. Looks at **Elizabeth***.*

John   You should be ashamed of yourself. Feeding off people's grief. Telling them there's some nirvana at the end where it'll all *make sense* and we'll all understand –

Mary   She never said that –

John (*to* **Elizabeth**)   I'd like you to leave.

Mary   I invited her here.

John   OK, I'll go.

Mary   John, please stay –

John   I don't want to talk about this.

He goes out, slightly unsteadily.

Joe   Dad . . .

He follows him out. **Mary** *looks at* **Elizabeth***, helplessly.*

Mary   I'm sorry.

Elizabeth   You should have told them. You told me you'd discussed it.

Mary   I meant to. I tried.

Pause.

I'm not asking them to excuse her. I'm not asking them to like her, or feel sorry for her. Jesus, I can't tell you some of the thoughts I've had. One night I dreamt I was chasing her along Old Compton Street, and I managed to grab her by the hair, and as she fell, her face looked up at me, white and smooth like an egg. So I stamped on her head and it *was* an egg, and there was a little bloody foetus there, amongst the yolk and bits of shell. What does that mean, d'you think?

Elizabeth   Probably that you wanted to kill her. Reasonably enough.

Mary   If it was your child who died, would you want to kill her?

Elizabeth   Yes.

Mary   Why d'you do this?

Elizabeth   What?

Mary   The prison stuff.

Elizabeth   Not because I'm a saint.

Mary   Good. I hate saints.

Elizabeth   My brother was put away for dealing. I used to visit him. And I got to like prisons. His, anyway – which was fairly enlightened. Does that sound odd?

Mary   Yes.

Elizabeth   The people are great.

Mary   The prisoners?

Elizabeth   Lots of them. Yeah. Why shouldn't they be?

Mary   I never thought of it like that.

Elizabeth   The weird thing about prisons is, you walk through the door and there are all these people who've done terrible things, but also all these people who've done wonderful things. Middle-aged women teaching murderers about gamelan music. Vicars and rabbis and imams and shopkeepers, retired schoolteachers, minor aristocrats – plus fraudsters, killers, dealers, druggies, and people who won't pay their council tax – they're all there, organising choirs and photography workshops, book clubs, and God knows what else, for no money, no kudos, nobody knows about them. There's a whole world in there.

Mary   So prison's a bit like the Women's Institute, is that what you're trying to say?

Elizabeth   No, sorry, obviously, they're not all doing creative writing and anger management courses. Some of them are doing home-made tattoos and being thoroughly miserable. Just like the outside.

Mary   Good. I'm glad. Why should she be singing her head off in a choir when Dan's dead?

Elizabeth   I don't think she is in a choir somehow.

Mary   D'you know, I've imagined beating her to death with a baseball bat. I've imagined setting her on fire, shooting her, running her over in a tank. Things that scare me, things I've never felt before, never imagined before. There's this kaleidoscopic rage inside me, and I realise I could kill someone. She kills my son, so I kill her, I wipe her off the face of the earth. I could do it. Truly.

Elizabeth   I believe you.

Mary   I felt if I knew a bit more about her I might be able to see her as a human being. Because it's no good feeling like this, it's killing me. Feeling like a murderer is killing me.

Silence.

Can I show you a picture of him?

Elizabeth   I'd like that.

Mary *takes a photograph from a drawer.*

Mary   John put all the photos away after the . . . after it happened.

She hands the photograph to **Elizabeth***.*

Elizabeth   He's very handsome.

Mary   He was, wasn't he?

Elizabeth   He looks like his father.

Mary   We've still got all his clothes. My sister keeps telling me to give them away, but I can't. She thinks it's because I go into his room and stroke them, or something. But it's not that,

it's stupider than that. I can't get rid of his clothes because I
keep thinking he might need them. When he comes back.
I know, of course, that he's not coming back. But there's some
fathomless part of my brain that won't accept it. It doesn't
seem to be processed properly. And then I look at his shoes,
and they're still, you know, moulded to the shape of his feet.
You can see the shape of each toe, imprinted there on the
insole, the soft pad of his heel. And it seems somehow wrong
to throw that last bit of him away because we'll never see his
feet again. He actually had a very beautiful feet.

Silence.

Elizabeth   After the – after what happened –

Mary   You can say murder.

Elizabeth   Is that what you say?

Mary   Sometimes. Sometimes I just call it I call it 'it'. Or
'the'. After the . . . Before the . . .

Elizabeth   Yes.

Mary   Some people call it 'the thing'. The thing that
happened. Killing, and murder, they're literally unspeakable.
You watch people trying to form the words. As if they're
talking through shards of glass. John couldn't even say 'dead'
for the first few months.

Elizabeth   How is he coping now?

Mary   You saw him. What do you think?

Elizabeth   It's normal. What he's doing is normal.

Mary   When he's not running, he's in his shed. A kind of
office thing in the garden.

Elizabeth   What does he do there?

Mary   Nothing. I spied on him once from the upstairs
bedroom and he was sitting bolt upright, staring at the wall.
When I looked back an hour later he was still there. Still
staring at the wall.

Pause.

I think he'd shoot her, you know, if he met her. If he had a gun with him.

Elizabeth   *Does* he have a gun?

Mary   God, no. But he used to be in CND. And now he's pure Old Testament. He'd like to smite and scourge and turn her into a pillar of salt.

Elizabeth   Wouldn't you?

Mary   It won't bring him back, will it? I can say that even though I'm still expecting him to walk through the door at any minute. The college rang up a couple of months ago to ask if he was still taking up his place next year, and d'you know what I said? I said, 'Yes.' Because it seemed too premature to say he was dead. And too cruel. My parents are dead. Shakespeare's dead. The Queen Mother. But I can't seem to put Dan into that category, with all those dead people.

Pause.

I realise this is completely mad. Dead people are dead. They don't go to college. But I can't help it. I still think he might.

Pause.

What's she like?

Elizabeth   Emma Price?

Mary   She looked normal in court. Not vicious or threatening, or mad. Normal.

Elizabeth   She is and she isn't.

Mary   Meaning?

Elizabeth   On the one hand she's completely normal and on the other she killed your son. Which is not really a normal thing to do.

Mary   So she's what? Mad?

Elizabeth   You could say damaged, I suppose.

Mary   I know all about damage. Everywhere I turn I hit a
blank where Dan used to be. The fridge is full of the food he
liked, those plastic cheese slices, bright pink yogurt. Joe won't
eat them. Why am I still buying this stuff? It's as if I'm saying,
don't worry, you may be dead but I'm still taking care of you.

Pause.

Does she have any idea what she's done? The stupid, ignorant,
selfish – I looked at her in court and she looked about twelve.
I could strangle her. I could beat her to a pulp. I wish she had
never been born. She's a waste of space, she's using up resources
that could be put to better use. I mean, what is the point of
her being alive? Why should she be walking around breathing
when Dan is ashes in an urn?

*She looks round the room and takes a pot from a cupboard. Bangs it on the
table.*

There. That's Dan. That's the son I gave birth to. That's what
she's done. And even like that he's a better person than she will
ever be.

She takes the lid off the pot, and takes out a handful of ash.

I thought it would be just grey, but look, it glints in the light,
there are flashes of green and blue, like jewels, can you see
them? Look how he catches the light, even now.

Pause.

We don't know what to do with him. So he sits here on a shelf.
And every so often I take him down and run him through my
fingers.

*She looks at **Elizabeth**.*

Mary   I had an idea the other day. I thought I'd mix him in
with the muesli, and I'd eat a bit of him every day, and for
some deranged reason, this was very comforting to me. I mean,
he's my son, he was inside me once before, he'd be coming
home, in a way. It seemed quite logical. And then it occurred
to me that they'd lock me up if I did that.

She puts the ashes back in the pot.

Look at what she's done to me, she's turned me into this person I don't recognise, she's turned me into a person I hate, who's seriously considering eating the ashes of her dead son. How could one stupid, inconsequential, vicious girl do so much damage?

Pause.

I'll never forgive her.

Pause.

Ever.

Elizabeth   No. Why should you?

Mary   That's what John and Joe are afraid of. They think I'm asking them to do that, and I never would. Before it was John, Joe, Dan and me. Now it's John, Joe, me and Emma Price. And I thought I needed to know something about her, even if I do want to kill her.

She rummages through her bag.

I got our lawyer to get the social worker's report. The one the judge took into account when he sentenced her.

She takes out a sheet of paper and hands it to **Elizabeth**.

Mary   Read it and tell me what you think

Elizabeth   Now?

Mary   Yes.

Elizabeth (*reading*)   'Emma Price. Born 27 May 1989, in Bethnal Green. Mother, Anne Marie, nineteen at the time of her birth, already had eighteen-month-old twins, one of whom had recently died. Cause of death listed as cot death. Twins' father not named, Emma's father named as Jason Price, but doesn't seem to have been much in evidence during childhood. When Emma was two her mother married someone called Damien Wilkins, had another child, boy named Franklin. Marriage broke up soon afterwards. Two years after that, her

mother married again, much older man named Mick Harris.
Two children from this marriage, which ended when Mick was
sent to prison for fourteen years for armed robbery. Mother
subsequently had several relationships, twice hospitalised
because of domestic violence. Emma lived variously with
mother, maternal grandmother, next-door neighbour, a second
cousin, and was briefly, aged seven, taken into care. Mother
had drug- and alcohol-related problems, but otherwise an
adequate mother.'

Pause.

Mary   Did you know any of this?

Elizabeth   Some of it.

Mary   So is that why?

Elizabeth   Why what?

Mary   She did it.

Elizabeth   It's just a list of historical facts. It might explain
some things, it might not.

Mary   A bad upbringing's not an excuse.

Elizabeth   No. It's not. But –

Mary   There are no buts.

Pause.

Elizabeth   What is it that you want, Mary? You've obviously
gone to enormous trouble to get this report, to track me down –

Mary   I want to . . . understand.

Elizabeth   You can't say 'I want to understand' on the one
hand and 'I will never change how I feel about this' on the
other. Understanding *will* change how you feel. It always does.
That's the point of understanding, isn't it?

Mary   I can see that. I'm not stupid.

Elizabeth   This is a long road you're choosing to go down.
You might feel better about certain things, but you'll probably

feel worse about others. And I wish I could say you'll feel
better at the end of it, but it's possible you won't.

Mary   In 1989 Dan was born in Chiswick. Two months
later, Emma Price was born in Bethnal Green. They never met
each other until she stabbed him to death. I need to piece
together how this came about. I need to understand how those
two lives collided so catastrophically.

Elizabeth   OK.

Mary   What did you *really* make of her? When you met her?

Elizabeth   She was pretty quiet in the workshops. Hard to
draw out.

Mary   What did she say?

Elizabeth   Absolutely nothing at all for the whole eight weeks.
Apart from yes and no. But she'd chosen to come, nobody
forced her to do it. She must have come for a reason. At the
end of the very last session, when everyone else was leaving,
she asked me if I would see her sometimes. She'd never had
any visitors.

Mary   Why?

Elizabeth   Her mother's ill. She's not close to the rest of her
family.

Mary   How often d'you see her?

Elizabeth   Once a fortnight.

Mary   D'you like her?

Pause.

Elizabeth   I don't dislike her.

Mary   And she's very damaged?

Elizabeth   I'd say so.

Mary   Is she mentally ill?

Elizabeth   No. She's just completely fucked up. And I know this is not what you want to hear, but from time to time, she's also extremely funny.

Pause.

Mary   Funny?

Elizabeth   Yes.

Mary   Right.

Pause.

Funny. It's not what I was expecting. I don't associate 'funny' with . . . people like that.

Elizabeth   Like what?

Mary   Murderers. Which of course is ridiculous, I mean, they can't be in murder mode all the time, can they? They must do normal things like tell jokes and go to the supermarket. When they're not murdering people.

Elizabeth   It's not usually a lifestyle choice. Murder. More a moment of madness.

Pause.

Mary   So. She's funny, then, Emma Price.

Elizabeth   Yes.

Mary   Dan was funny.

Elizabeth   Was he?

Mary   I don't suppose he'd find this very amusing though. Not many laughs in sudden, premature, violent death. Still, it hasn't spoilt *her* sense of humour, apparently. The little fucker.

Blackout.

Lights up on **John**, *with a glass of whisky.*

John   I'm not pissed. I just need something to take the edge off, because I've done my knee in and I can't run. To be honest, I am putting away a bit more than I used to, but I don't know how to do this stone-cold sober. Before it happened, we were a tight little family. We were a unit. It wasn't *Little House on the Prairie*, but we were solid. And now there are cracks appearing everywhere, huge fissures opening up, crevices where there were none before. Joe thinks Dan was our favourite, but he wasn't. He wasn't.

Pause.

It's just . . . Dan carried all our hopes and they died with him. He was the clever one. He was going to be a lawyer, I felt he was going to be a better version of me, the me I'd liked to have been. But that's not to say that we don't love Joe just as much. It's just . . . I'm ashamed of this, I really am, I hate myself, but I feel the future died with Dan. And I know I shouldn't feel it, I know it's wrong. We still have Joe and thank God for that, but I can't help it. Everything's been chipped away from our family and all the fault lines exposed, all the nerves. No one should have to go through this. And now Mary wants us to talk about the girl that did it to us. Why? I want to wipe her off the face of the earth, I don't want to spend a single moment of my life thinking about this woman, I want her not to exist, I don't want to hear her name, as far as I'm concerned she hasn't got a name. What does she mean, we have to talk about her? What good will that do? I'm not interested in people in prison, they've nothing to do with me, they're criminals, they've wrecked people's lives and I refuse to think about them.

Pause.

I don't know where this stuff comes from actually. It doesn't even feel like me talking. I'm saying things I find . . . hateful. Hate-full. Full of hate. That's what I've become. I've become a person I despise. I can feel it like battery acid, corroding me. And I hate that too. I hear this venom coming from my mouth and I think who is this speaking, it's not me, I'm trapped inside, a tiny diminished me, not much more than a speck really, waving a desperate semaphore. I went to the doctor last week and I said I've got this pain in my chest, just here, and he said that's your heart, and I said I know it's my fucking heart, I know it is. Why did I imagine there was a pill I could take? Why did I think he could take the pain away? The only time it goes away is when briefly, for a moment, I imagine shooting her.

Blackout.

Lights up on **Emma**, *sitting at a table talking to* **Elizabeth**. **Emma** *is unnaturally chirpy.*

Emma   If there's one thing I'm an expert on it's drugs. I could do a degree in drugs, I'd get honours. Dope, crack, coke, uppers, downers, little jelly things I don't even know what they were, I'd take anything, bottles of cough mixture, my nan's sleeping pills, and I loved vodka, I don't know if it's classified as a drug, is it?

Elizabeth   Not really, although −

Emma   I loved it. And whisky, I'd drink that. Chivas Regal. Cinzano. Tanqueray Gin. I love all the names. Noilly Prat, ever had that? I've always had exotic tastes. Can't stand alcopops, although I mean I would if there was nothing else going. But I wouldn't choose them, you know? Have you ever had a drink called Dubonnet?

Elizabeth   My grandmother used to drink it.

Emma   I found some in this old woman's flat, I was looking after her cat. I showed it to my nan and she said that's Dubonnet, it's delicious. And it was.

Elizabeth   Which old woman was that?

Emma   I can't remember. She lived upstairs.

Elizabeth   When?

Emma   I found a bottle of this other stuff once, it was called something like Suze. I showed it to my nan, she said it's French. I used to know a girl called Suze, she was mental. This was made from some sort of vegetable, artichokes I think, or maybe it was some sort of herb, anyway it's bright yellow like piss and it makes you wince, but actually after a couple of glasses it's quite nice. Actually it might not have been artichoke. It sounds like a disease, doesn't it? Artichoke. Ever had it?

Elizabeth   The disease?

Emma   It's not a disease, I told you, it's a vegetable. You can eat it. But this was a drink.

Elizabeth   It sounds disgusting.

Emma   It's all right if you mix it with a big bottle of Coke. I had it when I was about eight, I nicked a shopping bag in Selfridges when I was bunking off and there it was. Sixty Silk Cut, a box of cheese straws, a bottle of brandy and a bottle of Suze. Oh, and a packet of Pampers. Some alcoholic must have nicked a kid. I've never seen Suze again. You ever seen it?

Elizabeth   No, I –

Emma   I'm an expert on all the things that blow your head off, fuck your brain up, and make you feel nice and woozy. I've been drinking since I was six, no kidding. Had my first spliff when I was eight, nicked it from my mum's friend, I can't remember his name, but he was sort of like my dad at the time. It didn't make me sick or anything, and I smoked the whole thing. Yeah. I've always been advanced for my age.

Pause.

You don't believe me, do you?

Elizabeth   Were you close to your nan? You mention her a lot.

Emma   What's that drink called? It's bright blue.

Elizabeth   Whereas you hardly ever mention your mother.

Emma   You think I'm not going to drink that, it's a weird colour, nothing you eat's blue, is it?

Elizabeth   No.

Emma   Or maybe there is something. Can you think of anything?

Elizabeth   No.

Emma   Smarties. Can you get blue Smarties?

Elizabeth   Possibly.

Emma   It's not natural, though, is it? Smarties aren't a natural product. You don't, like, grow them, do you?

Elizabeth   No. But your point is?

Emma   I dunno, oh yeah, Cura-something, that's what it's called.

Elizabeth   What?

Emma   This drink. The blue one. I can't pronounce it. I drank a whole bottle! I bet you think that's impossible, don't you? How d'you think I did it?

Elizabeth   Curaçao.

Emma   What?

Elizabeth   Blue Curaçao. That's the name of drink.

Emma   You mix it with Coke and you can't tell it's blue. It's only the colour that puts you off. D'you see?

Elizabeth   Very ingenious.

Emma   Yeah. If you ever need advice on cocktails, I'm the person to come to.

Elizabeth   What happened to your arm?

Emma   I could write a book on cocktails, that would be a laugh, seriously though, I could, why shouldn't I, that girl off *Big Brother* wrote a book, you know who I mean?

Elizabeth   I was just asking about your arm.

Emma   There's only one thing that bothers me about this place: it doesn't have a bar. I mean, I know you can't have a bar in a prison, we'd all be off our faces, and me I'd be getting into trouble because when I've had a few I can get a bit you know, but I miss it, it's the only thing I miss, the absolute only thing.

Elizabeth   There's a bandage sticking out from your sleeve. I can see it. There. What's that?

Emma   Oh, yeah. It's a bandage.

Elizabeth   What happened?

Emma   Cut myself.

Elizabeth   How?

Emma   God, shut up will you?

Elizabeth   How did you cut yourself?

Emma   I was depressed.

Elizabeth   You did it on purpose?

Emma   I'm fine. I've got no problems.

Elizabeth   Have you done this before?

Emma   Jesus Christ, what fucking planet are you living on, of course I've done it before you stupid cunt.

Silence.

Well, you are. Stupid fucking question.

Elizabeth   I think –

Emma   Go on then, piss off, I know you're dying to get away.

Elizabeth   I'm not.

Emma   Well, you're an arse then. What d'you want to stay here for and be insulted?

Elizabeth   Is there anything you'd like me to bring you next time I come in?

Emma   You're coming back, are you?

Elizabeth   D'you want me to?

Emma   I wouldn't bother if I was you.

Elizabeth   D'you want me to?

Emma *shrugs.*

Emma   It's up to you.

Elizabeth   But would you like me to?

Emma   What d'you think I'm going to tell you?

Elizabeth   I'm sorry?

Emma   Are you waiting for me to tell you my life story?

Elizabeth   Isn't that what you've been doing?

Emma   I've not told you anything yet. I've just told you a lot of crap I made up.

Pause.

Elizabeth   Why did you ask me to visit you?

Emma   I can't remember. It must have seemed like a good idea at the time.

Pause.

D'you want to know about my nan then?

Elizabeth   D'you want to tell me?

Emma   She was great. She died though.

Elizabeth   How old were you when that happened?

Emma   She was a tiny little thing. Loved her booze. That's what killed her, I don't think she was that old, fifty or something, she would always give me a nip of something. Cherry brandy

I had off her once. She loved it with lemonade. And she always had these sweets, cherry lips, they were called, tasted like perfume, we used to eat whole handfuls. And liquorice allsorts. Jelly babies. Toblerones. We used to sit there watching *Countdown* with a huge glass of rum and Coke each, and a Toblerone. It was gorgeous. I thought I was really sophisticated. Getting pissed with my granny, aged nine. Fucking mental if you think about it.

Pause.

And then she went and died. She used to say, just a tiny drop of rum for you, you're only little, and then she'd give me a huge great slug of it. I don't thinks she understood measures and that. One of the first binge drinkers, my nan. She was a laugh though. And then she went and died. Which is the reason I became a junkie streetwalker with a knife in my pocket and the reason I ended up in here.

Elizabeth   Really?

Emma   Nah. That would be the film though, wouldn't it? 'Tormented childhood and death of grandmother turns girl into killer.'

Elizabeth   So what d'you think the real reason might be?

Emma   Haven't a clue. Probably I'm quite a bad person.

Elizabeth   Is that what you think?

Emma   What am I in here for?

Elizabeth   Sorry?

Emma   What crime?

Elizabeth   Murder.

Emma   Exactly. Murder. A very bad thing. I'm a danger to the community. A very bad person. I'm a violent criminal. I'm evil.

Elizabeth   Is that what you think?

Emma   What?

Elizabeth   That you're evil?

Emma   I dunno. Why?

Elizabeth   That's what you just said.

Emma   I'll say anything, me.

Elizabeth   If I said that his mother wanted to contact you, what would you say?

Emma   Whose mother?

Elizabeth   Daniel Pritchard's.

Emma   Who's he?

Elizabeth   You know who he is.

Pause.

Emma   Why? Why would she want to do that?

Elizabeth   She just wants to make contact, that's all.

Emma   Why?

Elizabeth   Have you anything against it in principle?

Emma   I don't know.

Pause.

What's she going to do, shout at me?

Elizabeth   I don't know.

Emma *gets up.*

Emma   I have to go. You can bring me some cigarettes next time, if you want.

She goes. Blackout.

Lights up on **Mary**, **Joe** *and* **John**. *They're sitting at a table, with a cloth on it. They've just finished supper.* **John** *is drunk. There's a bottle of whisky next to him and a glass at his elbow. The atmosphere is strained.*

Mary   That was nice, wasn't it?

Silence.

Being together. As a family.

Silence.

Joe   Can I go out now?

Mary   Just sit here . . . a few minutes. That's all.

Joe   Why?

Mary   I'm trying – A family should – we should eat together –

Joe   We just have. Can I go now?

Mary   It's important.

Joe   We never did this when Dan was alive. Why do we have to do it now?

Mary   Tell him, John.

John   Tell him what?

Mary   Why we need to sit down together once a day as a family.

John   Let him go if he wants to.

Joe   Thanks, Dad.

He goes. **Mary** *gets up to clear the table.*

John   Sit down.

Mary   I'm just –

John   Sit down –

She does so. He fiddles around in his pocket and brings out a piece of paper.

John (*reading*)   'Dear Emma Price, My name is Mary Pritchard. Daniel Pritchard, the boy you killed, was my son. This is not a hate letter, so please don't throw it away. The only time I saw you was in court, and you looked so normal to have done such a terrible thing. And now you seem to be part of our lives, squatting in our family like a huge cuckoo. The fact is, I am haunted by you, and I know nothing about you. I wondered if you could write back to me and tell me a little about yourself? I realise you must think this very strange, but it would help me so much if you could do this. I need to understand what has happened. I need the whole story so that I can make sense of this senseless thing. Thank you very much. Mary Pritchard.'

She looks at him, afraid. He takes a large slug of whisky.

John   Were you actually going to send this?

Mary   I –

John   Because it's mad, this is the sort of thing a mad person does –

Mary   I'm entitled to madness.

John   No, no, please don't do this.

Mary   I have no illusions about it. I'm not expecting closure, whatever the hell that is, I'm not expecting to move on anywhere –

John   You were actually going to send it?

Mary   I – yes – I –

John   What were you expecting her to say? Sorry?

Mary   For God's sake, John, d'you want to keep running for the rest of your life –

John   I've stopped running.

Mary   You're getting through four bottles of whisky a week! You're still running away. I can't tell if you're running from it or me, you're never sober enough to tell me! I used to get into bed and you'd set off round the block for *a jog* and come back three hours later. Now I get into bed and you're downstairs in front of the telly with a bottle of whisky –

John   While you're up there writing love letters to a murderer –

Mary   Oh don't talk crap, you know nothing, you understand *nothing* –

John *hits her across the face. She hits him back. They've never hit each other before. They both reel.* **Joe** *appears.*

Joe   I forgot my – What happened?

John *and* **Mary** *are both in tears.*

John   Nothing. It's over.

He goes to **Mary**.

John   Sorry. I'm so sorry.

Joe   What did you do?

Mary   We – nothing – there was a disagreement –

John   I hit her. I hit her. I'm sorry.

Joe   Jesus Christ, Dad, what's happening? What are you doing to each other?

Mary   It's OK –

Joe   It's not OK! D'you want to know what's happened? The most important person in this house, the person behind every thought, every impulse, every daydream or screaming match, is Danny. A dead person. A dead person is in charge of our lives.

Mary   Joe –

Joe   Why don't you ask me what I want occasionally? Go on, ask me. I'll tell you. I'd like to be considered as important as my little brother, who happens to be dead. I'd like parity with the stiff, if that's not too much to ask. In fact, I'll go further than that. I'd like be considered *more* important. Because the great thing about me is that I'm actually breathing, which

I think gives me the edge over a kilo and a half of ash sitting in a tub on the kitchen shelf.

Silence.

Or maybe you disagree?

John *tries to speak, but can't.*

John   I – I – that's not –

He turns away and goes out.

Joe   What is his problem?

Mary   Leave him alone, Joe, please.

Pause.

Joe   What happened?

Mary   He found a letter I wrote to Emma Price. He thinks I want to forgive her or something.

Joe   Do you?

Mary   I don't know what I want.

Pause.

I want to be free.

Joe   Of what?

Mary   As long as I'm shackled to her I'm shackled to Danny's murder, and he was more than that. He was more than just a violent death.

Joe   So what are you going to do about it?

Mary   I thought you were going out? Go on, you need to get out of here –

Joe   Why did he hit you?

Mary   I hit him back, by the way.

Joe   You've never hit each other. Ever.

Mary He's trying to deal with Danny being killed his way, and I'm trying to deal with it my way. And the problem is, my way makes him want to kill me, too.

Blackout.

Lights up on **Emma** *and* **Elizabeth**. **Emma** *is holding a letter which* **Elizabeth** *has just handed over.*

Emma Who's it from?

Elizabeth Mary Pritchard.

Emma Who's she?

Elizabeth Daniel Pritchard's mother. I told you about her.

A beat.

Emma What does she want?

Elizabeth Why don't you read it and see?

Emma No thanks.

She tries to hand it back to **Elizabeth**.

Elizabeth It's addressed to you. Keep it. You might want to read it later.

Emma I won't.

Elizabeth Keep it anyway.

Emma What does she want?

Elizabeth Why don't you read the letter?

Emma Why don't you tell me?

Elizabeth She asked me to give it to you.

Emma I don't want it.

Elizabeth Is that what you'd like me to tell her?

Emma   Tell her anything you like.

Elizabeth   OK.

Silence.

Emma   Did you bring my fags?

Elizabeth   Yes.

She rummages in her bag and takes out a pack of cigarettes.

I couldn't get the Rolos. They didn't have any.

Emma   Where?

Elizabeth   At my local shop.

Emma   Must be a pretty poxy shop.

Elizabeth   Well, they didn't have any.

Emma   Get Rolos anywhere. Poxiest shop on earth sells Rolos.

Elizabeth   This one doesn't.

Emma   Cos it's poxy.

Elizabeth   Are you going to read the letter or not?

Emma   You could have got me a bar of fruit and nut instead.

Elizabeth   I'll leave it with you.

Emma   Or a packet of Starbursts.

Elizabeth   You can read it later.

Emma   Starbursts used to be called Opal Fruits. Did you know that?

Elizabeth   Yes.

Emma   A KitKat would've done. Fuck's sake. What's a KitKat cost? Nothing. Have a break, have a KitKat.

Elizabeth *puts the letter on the table between them.*

Elizabeth   I'll leave it here, OK?

Emma   Stop going on about the fucking letter, will you?

Elizabeth   Stop going on about fucking confectionary.

Pause.

Emma   I've never heard you swear before.

Elizabeth   Well, now you have.

Emma   Anyway, I like confectionary. Or sweets as I call them.

Elizabeth   I'll get you a KitKat the next time.

Emma   You coming back then?

Elizabeth   What d'you mean?

Emma   Why d'you bother? I'm a waste of time.

Elizabeth   No you're not.

Emma   I fucking am.

Elizabeth   You can certainly be very trying.

Emma (*impersonating her*)   'You can certainly be very trying.'

Elizabeth   That's not a very nice thing to do, Emma.

Emma   'That's not a very nice thing to do, Emma.'

Elizabeth   Look, we can waste this visit, or we can make it worthwhile, it's up to you.

Emma   I don't give a fuck, I never asked you to visit me.

Elizabeth   Actually you did.

Emma   I don't even like you, you're a cunt with a stupid voice, I even hate what you look like and you don't smell right, you smell fucking terrible, has no one ever told you that?

Elizabeth *is unfazed. She says nothing.*

Emma   Have you ever eaten out of a dustbin?

Elizabeth   No.

Emma   I have.

Elizabeth   Really.

Emma   I was hungry.

Elizabeth *says nothing.*

Emma   You don't believe me, do you?

Elizabeth   Why d'you think that might be?

Emma   I was eight or nine. My brother and me used to go round the bins. One time we found half a birthday cake, just with a bit of ash on it.

Elizabeth   You must have been very hungry.

Emma   Ha ha, I was only joking.

Elizabeth   Were you?

Emma   Guess.

Elizabeth   You were hungry. Why?

Emma   Because no one fed us because my nan was in hospital.

Elizabeth   Where was your mother?

Emma   Off somewhere.

Elizabeth   Where?

Emma   I can't remember. She used to go out and not come back. But she must have gone for ages this time because there was nothing in the house to eat and we didn't have any money so we went round the bins.

Elizabeth   I'm so sorry. That must have been horrible.

Emma   Yeah, it was pretty poxy. You feel a right charlie. Yeah.

Pause.

My nan used to say that. 'A right charlie.'

Elizabeth   Was there no one you could have gone to?

Emma   My nan, but she was in hospital, I told you.

Elizabeth   How long did this go on for?

Emma   I can't remember now. I think the woman next door took us into her place and gave us some baked beans.

Pause.

I know what you're thinking, I bet you think I'm going to go whining on again about my rubbish childhood and everything, but I'm not, I mean, it can't have been that bad, can it, or I'd be dead. Like my brother. Someone shot him, I'm not kidding. It's ridiculous, it's like a joke my family, you couldn't put us on the telly, no one would believe it, we've got drugs, shootings, being on the game, broken noses, social services, horrible sex stuff and half the time the electric's cut off. We're one of those families you read about in the papers, the judge said my background was pitiful. Rude bastard. He's right, mind you. I just don't think he should've said it in public, in front of people, you don't want everyone to know your mum was on the game and your grandad was a kiddie fiddler, it's not your fault.

Elizabeth   No, it's not your fault.

Emma   OK, which bit of what I just said's not true?

Elizabeth   Most of it?

Emma   Which bit? Guess.

Elizabeth   I've no idea.

Emma   Because you see the other thing they said about me is I'm a bit of fantasist.

Elizabeth   Yes.

Emma   D'you think I am?

Elizabeth   I think you make things up.

Emma   Not everything. Some of what I say's true.

Elizabeth   I know.

Emma   Ha-ha! Which bit?

Elizabeth   I'm not sure.

Pause.

Emma   This woman who wrote me the letter.

Elizabeth   Mary Pritchard.

Emma   What's she want?

Elizabeth   I don't know.

Emma   Why not?

Elizabeth   Because the letter's addressed to you, not me.

Emma   Didn't you ask her what she wrote?

Elizabeth   No.

Emma   I'd have sneaked a look at it.

Pause.

What d'you think she wants then?

Elizabeth   Why don't you just read it and see?

Pause.

Emma   He was rude to me. Very fucking rude.

Elizabeth   Who was?

Emma   He made me really pissed off.

Elizabeth   Daniel Pritchard?

Emma   He didn't need to tell me to fuck off.

Elizabeth   You didn't need to stab him.

Emma   He grabbed my tit.

Elizabeth   You didn't need to stab him.

Emma   I was off my face, I was not in possession of my faculties. And he was a fucking rude bastard.

Elizabeth   You don't kill people because they're rude.

Emma   I did though, didn't I?

Elizabeth   And you were –

Emma   Coked out of my head.

Elizabeth   So you asked him for money. He said fuck off and you stabbed him.

Emma   Yeah.

Elizabeth   What was going through your head?

Emma   I can't remember. I was –

Elizabeth   Out of your head.

Emma   Yeah.

She gets up.

Anyway. See you.

Elizabeth   Are you off?

Emma   Yeah. See you.

Elizabeth   OK.

Emma   Go on then. Bye.

Elizabeth   I'll see you next time, yes?

Emma   If you want.

Elizabeth *turns to go.*

Emma (*holding it out*)   You forgot your letter.

Elizabeth   It's not my letter, it's yours.

She goes. **Emma** *looks at the letter for a long time. She puts it in her pocket without opening it.*

Blackout.

Lights up on **Mary**, **John** *and* **Elizabeth**.

John   I don't care if she had a rubbish childhood, *I* had a rubbish childhood and I don't go around stabbing strangers because they won't give me the money for crack or heroin or whatever it was. Her dad was a sadistic arsehole? That's not a reason, it's not an excuse, fuck the mitigating circumstances, *my* dad was a sadistic arsehole –

Mary   No he wasn't, you just made that up.

John   – and I don't go around killing people –

Mary   Well, good for you. What is the point of comparing yourself to this girl? What are you trying to say? That you're a better person? We know that –

John   Of course I'm better than a murderer!

Mary   I can't believe we're having this argument, it's absurd –

John   You started it –

Elizabeth *gets up.*

Elizabeth   Look, I'm going to go, and you can call me later in the week when you've sorted out what it is you want to do. If anything.

John   Good idea.

Mary   Sit down, he doesn't mean it.

John   Yes I do.

Elizabeth   Look, for what it's worth, I don't think you should visit Emma. Yet.

John   You think she's going to be grateful for your forgiveness or something, but all it's going to do is rake up more grief and more pain –

Mary   I never said I was going to forgive her. I just believe she might – it might give her the chance to – I don't know . . . she might . . . say sorry . . .

John   Oh, don't be so fucking ridiculous!

Mary   It's not impossible, is it, Elizabeth?

Elizabeth   Well . . . I wouldn't bank on it . . .

John   You see?

Elizabeth   I mean, obviously it's not impossible –

Mary   That's not the reason I'm doing it.

Elizabeth   I actually think Emma and I are getting somewhere. But she can't apologise until she completely understands what she's done, d'you see?

John   She killed someone. She went to prison. What's *not* to understand?

Mary   I know what I'm doing, and I know you don't, but I'm going to meet her. You can stay in the dark, but I'm walking towards the light.

Blackout.

Lights up on **Mary** *and* **Emma**. *Visiting time.*

Mary   Hello.

She stares at **Emma**.

Emma   Hi.

Pause.

Mary   How are you?

Emma   Fine.

Pause.

Mary   Good . . .

Pause.

Thank you for agreeing to meet me.

Emma   Whatever.

Mary   I'm glad you did.

Pause.

Are you?

Emma   Am I what?

Mary   Glad. That we could meet.

Emma *shrugs.*

Mary   You weren't nervous?

Emma   What about?

Mary   Meeting me.

Emma   It doesn't bother me.

Mary   Doesn't it?

Emma   No.

Pause.

Mary   Danny was our youngest son.

Emma   Yeah.

Mary   We have another son called Joe. He's twenty.

Emma   Right.

Mary   Danny was about to go to university.

Emma   Good for him.

Elizabeth *appears with three polystyrene cups of tea.*

Elizabeth   Three teas.

Emma   I don't want tea.

Elizabeth   So don't drink it.

Emma   I wanted coffee.

Elizabeth   Well, I –

Emma   Forget it. It doesn't matter.

Mary   Please. Get her a coffee, could you?

Elizabeth   Sure.

She goes.

Emma   Why did you do that?

Mary   I suppose I'm trying to show that I mean you no harm.

Emma   Why?

Elizabeth   Because . . . I don't. Mean you any harm.

Emma   You fucking mental?

Elizabeth   What d'you mean?

Emma   Nothing. Forget it.

Silence.

Mary   How are you . . . how are you finding it?

Emma   What?

Mary   Prison.

Emma   It's fine. I don't have a problem with it.

Mary   It must be very difficult being away from your family.

Emma   You haven't met my family.

Mary   No.

Emma   Right. Is that it then? Can I go now?

Mary   I've only just got here.

Emma   What d'you want me to say?

Mary   I don't know.

Emma   What you doing here then?

Mary   I don't know.

Emma   Jesus Christ . . .

Mary   Elizabeth's gone to get you a coffee, you can't go yet.

Emma   Elizabeth's a wanker.

Silence.

Mary   You read my letters?

Emma   No.

Mary   Why not?

Emma   I've been busy.

Mary   With what?

Elizabeth *comes back with the coffee.*

Elizabeth   Here we are.

Mary   What have you been busy with?

Emma   Bring any sugar?

Elizabeth *puts the sugar on the table.* **Emma** *puts three in her coffee.*

Emma   I love sugar.

Mary   You said you've been busy.

Emma   I love anything sweet. I can eat a whole box of Coco Pops. Not those tinsy ones from the variety pack. A big huge family one. In one sitting. I like sweets, sugar, chocolate, anything like that I can eat, but you know what I can't eat, olives, what is the point of an olive, I mean what is it, it tastes like shit, who invented the olive –

Elizabeth   Emma –

Emma   What?

Elizabeth   Mary doesn't want to hear one of your food rants –

Emma   But what *is* an olive?

Mary   It's a fruit.

Emma   It's not a fucking fruit.

Elizabeth   It doesn't matter what olives are, we've established you don't like them, so can we move on –

Emma   An orange is a fruit. An apple. An olive is like a piece of shit.

Elizabeth   Emma, come on –

Emma   A pineapple is a fruit. A lime. Lime's my favourite flavour. I love lime Starbursts. But can you imagine, right, an *olive*-flavoured Starburst? No, right, because a) it would be disgusting, and b) an olive is not a fruit.

Elizabeth   Let's get over the olives, can we?

Emma   OK.

Pause.

But it's not a fruit though.

Elizabeth   Fine.

Pause.

Emma   Why doesn't she just tell me what she wants?

Mary   I don't want anything.

Emma   So what's she doing here then?

Mary   Perhaps if you read the letters –

Elizabeth   You told me you *had* read them –

Mary   D'you still have the letters, Emma?

Emma   Yeah, somewhere.

Mary   Why is it you won't read them?

Emma *stares stonily ahead.*

Mary   Is it because you were frightened of what I might say in them?

Emma   No.

Mary   Is it –

Emma Look, I don't want to talk about the fucking letters, OK? I don't want to read them because whatever you have to say, I don't want to know, OK? I got no idea what you're doing here. Maybe you want to tell me how lovely your bloody son was, well, I hate to disappoint you he wasn't lovely he was a little shit. And I've got nothing to say to you, so piss off.

Mary *is shocked. She gets up.*

Elizabeth Mary –

Mary No. I made a mistake. I'm going.

Emma Good. And don't come back.

Mary Fine. I won't.

She goes.

Elizabeth What the hell was that about? Why did you do that? We'd been through this, we'd discussed every possibility, you told me you'd read those letters, what on earth were you doing?

Emma *fiddles with her fingers, says nothing.*

Elizabeth Can you imagine how much effort it took for her to come in here? Have you any idea what she's been through? Or d'you think it's all about you, is that it?

Emma She kept going on about the fucking letters.

Elizabeth Well, she did take the trouble to write them. The least you could do was to read them.

Emma I'm never going to bloody read them, OK?

Elizabeth OK, I give up. I can't believe what you've just done –

Emma I can't read them. D'you hear what I'm saying?

Elizabeth What d'you mean, you can't?

Emma I can't.

Pause.

Elizabeth   Oh.

Pause.

Why didn't you tell me this?

Emma   Because it's fucking embarrassing, why d'you think?

A beat.

Elizabeth   Does *anyone* know about it?

Emma   No.

Elizabeth   Oh, Emma . . .

Emma   I can do my name, though.

Elizabeth   That's good. That's a start.

Emma   And sometimes I look at newspapers and books and pretend. So someone says to me you want to read this book, it's great, and I go what's it about and they tell me and I go what's it called and they tell me and they lend it to me. And then I pretend I'm reading it, then I say to someone else, you want to read this book, it's great, and I tell them what it's about and everything.

Elizabeth   Have you kept the letters?

Emma   Yeah. Of course I have.

A beat.

No one's ever sent me a letter before.

Blackout.

Lights up on **Mary**. *She is sitting staring into space.* **John** *and* **Joe** *are with her.*

Mary   I should never have gone.

Pause.

Go on, say it. Say I told you so.

John   What happened?

Mary   She's horrible.

Joe   Like you thought she was going to be *lovable*?

Mary   In my head I saw myself . . . not forgiving, but . . . what? I don't know. Bestowing some sort of blessing on someone who doesn't exist. Certainly not the person I met.

John   What did she say?

Mary   She went on about olives.

Joe   Olives?

Mary   Is an olive a fruit or not.

John   It's a vegetable, isn't it?

Joe   It's a snack.

Mary   You see? You're doing it now.

John   How did you get onto olives in the first place?

Mary   No idea. Anyway. Then she said Danny was a little shit.

Joe   She didn't know him, Mum. She never met him.

John   She has to say that. Obviously. Because if he wasn't a shit why did she kill him?

Mary   She didn't read any of my letters, she called Dan a shit, she was rude, she didn't care. She has no concept of what she's done, or if she has she couldn't give a damn.

Silence.

Joe   Maybe you should give it another go, Mum.

John   No. It's too much. You tried. It's enough.

Joe   I'm just saying. Maybe her first instinct was right. Maybe she should go with it.

John   Look, can we just get something straight here. I'm prepared to admit the girl might have problems –

Joe   Well, what a fucking genius you are, Dad –

John   I know she must have things wrong in her life, of course I know that, but I don't seem to be able to care. I cannot care about it, or her, or her scabby childhood or anything else because every time I think about her I just see her putting a knife into Danny and every time I think about her he's killed again and so am I.

Pause.

And I just want us to forget her. Why can't we just forget her?

Joe   Because we're shackled to her, Dad. And Mum's trying to unshackle herself.

John   Because she's a better person than I am.

Joe   No.

John   I can't do what you're doing, Mary.

Mary   I'm not asking you to.

John   But it makes me feel like bad person. So you're cast as Mother Teresa and I'm Adolf Eichmann –

Mary   That is not what's happening –

John   When you saw her, what did you feel?

Mary   What?

John   She's sitting there in front of you. She killed your son. What did you feel?

Mary   I don't know . . . I was expecting rage, but no . . . Pity, I felt. And despair. Because she was so . . . ordinary. An ordinary cocky girl. And it made me feel like it didn't mean anything, that Dan was dead and it was just random and pointless and . . . ordinary –

She goes to the shelf, takes down the urn of ashes and slams it on the table.

Why didn't you value your life more? Why didn't you just give her the money? You should have died in bed at the age of eighty-five, you stupid – How could you do this to us, Dan, how could you be so careless, how can you be dead for nothing, you could have crossed the road, why couldn't you have just not been there –

She smashes the urn on the table.

Blackout.

Lights up on visiting time. **Mary**, **Emma** *and* **Joe**.

Mary   This is my son, Joe.

Emma   Hello.

Joe   Hi.

Mary   Joe was there. The night it – when it happened.

Emma   Right.

Mary   I wanted my husband to come too, but he won't. He can't do it. Not yet.

Emma *shrugs.*

Emma   Whatever.

Pause.

Mary   Anyway. How are you?

Emma   OK.

Pause.

Mary   Elizabeth told me about the letters.

Emma   Yeah.

Pause.

That's why – it wasn't – I just – I felt stupid or something.

Pause.

I'm sorry but this is really fucking weird. It's doing my head in.

Mary   Yes. It is weird.

Emma   I mean, you're sitting here with . . .

Joe   The person who killed her son. My brother.

Pause.

Emma   If I had my time over again I wouldn't have done it.

Mary   You're not going to have your time over again though, are you?

Emma   No. But I wouldn't have done it.

Pause.

Mary   Thank you.

Emma   But I did.

Mary   Yes.

Emma   I did do it.

Mary   Yes.

Emma   Fucking hell.

Pause.

So. There you go.

Pause.

I said he told me to fuck off and he did but loads of other people had said fuck off an' all, because I was probably being a bit of a pain.

Mary   OK.

Emma   I said he grabbed my tit.

Joe   Dan wouldn't have done that.

Pause.

Emma   Yeah. He didn't.

Mary   OK.

Emma   He didn't do anything.

Mary   So . . . ?

Emma   I don't know why I did it. I just . . . I was . . . angry or something . . . I didn't mean . . . I didn't think it would, you know, damage him so much . . .

Pause.

I didn't mean to ruin anyone's life.

Mary   What about your own?

Emma   Mine was rubbish to begin with.

Pause.

Did you hear me? I said I never meant it. I never meant to kill him.

Mary   Yes, I know, thank you.

Emma   Is that what you wanted to hear?

Mary   When I got here I thought I might tell you that I forgave you.

Pause.

Emma   You can't do that.

Mary   No. I can't. I could say it but I don't feel it.

Joe   I can't forgive you either.

Emma   So what do you want?

Mary   I thought . . . we thought . . . Joe and I – we thought it might be something we could . . . work towards.

Pause.

Emma   Are you taking the piss?

Mary   No.

Pause.

Did you bring the letters with you?

Emma   Yeah. D'you want them back or something?

Mary   I thought we could read them together.

Emma   I can't –

Mary   I know. We'll teach you.

Pause.

Emma   It's too late, isn't it?

Joe   No.

Pause.

Emma   OK . . .

Joe   When d'you want to start?

Emma *takes the letters from her pocket and pushes them across the table.*
Mary *opens the first one, and reads, pointing out the words to* **Emma**.

Mary   'Dear Emma Price, my name is Mary Pritchard.
Daniel Pritchard, the boy you killed, was my son . . . '

Fade down lights.

Spotlight on **Mary**.

Mary   I thought when I started this, that all I had to do was
say *I forgive you*, and the healing would start. But I can't say it.
Yet. Not truthfully anyway. It's a long road, I understand that
now. Sometimes I feel forgiveness and sometimes I don't.
Sometimes, I wake up in the morning and for a split second,
I forget that Dan is dead. And when I remember, it's as new
and harsh and as overwhelming as it was on that very first
morning. And I don't feel full of forgiveness and love, I feel
full of despair and anguish and fury at the person who did it.
Forgiveness wouldn't make the grief go away. That's what I've
learnt. I must have hoped it would, but when I started this I'd
no idea what I was doing. No one tells you how to do these

things, you don't expect you'll ever need to. So I'm groping along in the dark, as best I can.

Spotlight on **Joe**.

Joe My mum's much better at it than me. Sometimes I find it hard − you look at her and she's just this girl and she's even quite nice. So she's this quite nice girl who did this thing. This terrible thing. And I feel this rage coming up from deep down in my stomach, and I think it's going to burst from my throat. But I have to try and hold the two things side by side in my hands: the ordinary girl, the terrible thing. Because I think now, they're both true. They both have equal weight. One doesn't cancel out the other. Does it?

Spotlight on **John**.

John I can't do what they're doing. But I don't hold it against them any more. I'm on my road, they're on theirs. The house is calmer now. There seems to be some purpose to the day. I'm running again. It's pathological, I know, but it's better than whisky. The other day, Mary said to me, 'If you could have anything at this moment, what would it be? Something possible. Not Dan being alive.' And I couldn't answer at first, I couldn't think of anything. But then it came to me: dignity. I'd like for us to have some sort of dignity.

Pause.

I don't want people to think we're brave or pitiable, I don't want to be admired or healed, jollied along, moved on, cheered up and counselled. I just want . . . the grief to be accepted for itself, nothing more, nothing less. And I want to be allowed the dignity of carrying it, as best I can. Without flowers tied to lamp posts, and cuddly toys left in the rain. It's not a thing we value any more, but pain is something we must bear and we should be allowed to be proud in the bearing of it. I never really thought about it before. But dignity is what makes us human. Dignity gives us meaning. Dignity is as vital as air . . .

Spotlight on **Emma** *and* **Elizabeth**. **Emma** *is hesitantly reading a letter.*

Emma   ' . . . This is not a hate letter, so please don't throw it away. The only time I saw you was in court, and you looked so normal to have done such a terrible thing. And now you seem to be part of our lives, s— s— '

She struggles with the word. **Elizabeth** *looks at it*

Elizabeth   Squatting.

Emma   ' . . . squatting in our family like a huge cuckoo. The fact is, I am haunted by you, and I know nothing about you. I wondered if you could write back to me and tell me a little about yourself? I realise you must think this very strange, but it would help me so much if you could do this. I need to understand what has happened. I need the whole story so that I can make sense of this senseless thing. Thank you very much. Mary Pritchard.'

She looks up. **Elizabeth** *smiles at her.*

Blackout.

Methuen Drama Student Editions

Jean Anouilh *Antigone* • John Arden *Serjeant Musgrave's Dance*
Alan Ayckbourn *Confusions* • Aphra Behn *The Rover*
Edward Bond *Lear* • Bertolt Brecht *The Caucasian Chalk Circle*
Life of Galileo • *Mother Courage and her Children*
The Resistible Rise of Arturo Ui • *The Threepenny Opera*
Anton Chekhov *The Cherry Orchard* • *The Seagull* • *Three Sisters*
Uncle Vanya • Caryl Churchill *Serious Money* • *Top Girls*
Shelagh Delaney *A Taste of Honey* • Euripides *Elektra* • *Medea*
Dario Fo *Accidental Death of an Anarchist* • Michael Frayn *Copenhagen*
John Galsworthy *Strife* • Nikolai Gogol *The Government Inspector*
Robert Holman *Across Oka* • Henrik Ibsen *A Doll's House* • *Ghosts*
Hedda Gabler • Charlotte Keatley *My Mother Said I Never Should*
Bernard Kops *Dreams of Anne Frank* • Federico García Lorca
Blood Wedding • *Doña Rosita the Spinster* (bilingual edition) • *The House
of Bernarda Alba* • (bilingual edition) • *Yerma* (bilingual edition) • David
Mamet *Glengarry Glen Ross* • *Oleanna* • Patrick Marber *Closer* • John
Marston *The Malcontent* • Joe Orton *Loot* • Luigi Pirandello *Six
Characters in Search of an Author* • Mark Ravenhill *Shopping and
F***ing* • Willy Russell *Blood Brothers* • *Educating Rita* • Sophocles
Antigone • *Oedipus the King* • Wole Soyinka *Death and the King's
Horseman* • August Strindberg *Miss Julie* • J. M. Synge *The Playboy
of the Western World* • Theatre Workshop *Oh What a Lovely War*
Timberlake Wertenbaker *Our Country's Good* • Arnold Wesker *The
Merchant* • Oscar Wilde *The Importance of Being Earnest* • Tennessee
Williams *A Streetcar Named Desire* • *The Glass Menagerie*

Methuen Drama Modern Plays

include work by

Edward Albee
Jean Anouilh
John Arden
Margaretta D'Arcy
Peter Barnes
Sebastian Barry
Brendan Behan
Dermot Bolger
Edward Bond
Bertolt Brecht
Howard Brenton
Anthony Burgess
Simon Burke
Jim Cartwright
Caryl Churchill
Noël Coward
Lucinda Coxon
Sarah Daniels
Nick Darke
Nick Dear
Shelagh Delaney
David Edgar
David Eldridge
Dario Fo
Michael Frayn
John Godber
Paul Godfrey
David Greig
John Guare
Peter Handke
David Harrower
Jonathan Harvey
Iain Heggie
Declan Hughes
Terry Johnson
Sarah Kane
Charlotte Keatley
Barrie Keeffe
Howard Korder

Robert Lepage
Doug Lucie
Martin McDonagh
John McGrath
Terrence McNally
David Mamet
Patrick Marber
Arthur Miller
Mtwa, Ngema & Simon
Tom Murphy
Phyllis Nagy
Peter Nichols
Sean O'Brien
Joseph O'Connor
Joe Orton
Louise Page
Joe Penhall
Luigi Pirandello
Stephen Poliakoff
Franca Rame
Mark Ravenhill
Philip Ridley
Reginald Rose
Willy Russell
Jean-Paul Sartre
Sam Shepard
Wole Soyinka
Simon Stephens
Shelagh Stephenson
Peter Straughan
C. P. Taylor
Theatre de Complicite
Theatre Workshop
Sue Townsend
Judy Upton
Timberlake Wertenbaker
Roy Williams
Snoo Wilson
Victoria Wood

Methuen Drama Contemporary Dramatists

include

John Arden (two volumes)
Arden & D'Arcy
Peter Barnes (three volumes)
Sebastian Barry
Dermot Bolger
Edward Bond (eight volumes)
Howard Brenton
   (two volumes)
Richard Cameron
Jim Cartwright
Caryl Churchill
   (two volumes)
Sarah Daniels (two volumes)
Nick Darke
David Edgar (three volumes)
David Eldridge
Ben Elton
Dario Fo (two volumes)
Michael Frayn (three volumes)
John Godber (three volumes)
Paul Godfrey
David Greig
John Guare
Lee Hall (two volumes)
Peter Handke
Jonathan Harvey
   (two volumes)
Declan Hughes
Terry Johnson (three volumes)
Sarah Kane
Barrie Keeffe
Bernard-Marie Koltès
   (two volumes)
David Lan
Bryony Lavery
Deborah Levy
Doug Lucie

David Mamet (four volumes)
Martin McDonagh
Duncan McLean
Anthony Minghella
   (two volumes)
Tom Murphy (five volumes)
Phyllis Nagy
Anthony Neilson
Philip Osment
Gary Owen
Louise Page
Stewart Parker (two volumes)
Joe Penhall
Stephen Poliakoff
   (three volumes)
David Rabe
Mark Ravenhill
Christina Reid
Philip Ridley
Willy Russell
Eric-Emmanuel Schmitt
Ntozake Shange
Sam Shepard (two volumes)
Wole Soyinka (two volumes)
Simon Stephens
Shelagh Stephenson
David Storey (three volumes)
Sue Townsend
Judy Upton
Michel Vinaver
   (two volumes)
Arnold Wesker (two volumes)
Michael Wilcox
Roy Williams (two volumes)
Snoo Wilson (two volumes)
David Wood (two volumes)
Victoria Wood

Methuen Drama World Classics

include

Jean Anouilh (two volumes)
Brendan Behan
Aphra Behn
Bertolt Brecht (eight volumes)
Büchner
Bulgakov
Calderón
Čapek
Anton Chekhov
Noël Coward (eight volumes)
Feydeau
Eduardo De Filippo
Max Frisch
John Galsworthy
Gogol
Gorky (two volumes)
Harley Granville Barker
 (two volumes)
Victor Hugo
Henrik Ibsen (six volumes)
Jarry

Lorca (three volumes)
Marivaux
Mustapha Matura
David Mercer (two volumes)
Arthur Miller (five volumes)
Molière
Musset
Peter Nichols (two volumes)
Joe Orton
A. W. Pinero
Luigi Pirandello
Terence Rattigan
 (two volumes)
W. Somerset Maugham
 (two volumes)
August Strindberg
 (three volumes)
J. M. Synge
Ramón del Valle-Inclan
Frank Wedekind
Oscar Wilde